POP STAR

LISA REGAN

WINDMILL
BOOKS
New York

Published in 2013 by Windmill Books, An Imprint of Rosen Publishing
29 East 21st Street, New York, NY 10010

Produced for Windmill by Calcium Creative Ltd
Editors for Calcium Creative Ltd: Sarah Eason and Vicky Egan
US Editor: Sara Antill
Designer: Nick Leggett

Cover: Shutterstock: Holbox fg, DWPhotos bg. Inside: Dreamstime: Brian
Chase 7; Istockphoto: Kvonomax 1, Nicole S. Young 3br, 24; Shutterstock:
ArrowStudio, LLC 16–17, Arvzdix 10, Bettina Baumgartner 13, Uluc Ceylani
8, Christian Bertrand 5, Brocreative 18, Dooley Productions 23, Helga Esteb
27, 28, Fokusgood 15, Gelpi 14, 29, Holbox 20, Valeriy Lebedev 12, Martin
Lehmann 25, Nejron Photo 9, PASphotography 4, Photoproject.eu 21,
Photosindiacom LLC 26, Kiselev Andrey Valerevich 22, Vipflash 6, Debby
Wong 11, Zoom Team 19.

Library of Congress Cataloging-in-Publication Data

Regan, Lisa, 1971–
 Pop star / by Lisa Regan.
     p. cm. — (Stage school)
Includes index.
ISBN 978-1-4488-8096-6 (library binding) — ISBN 978-1-4488-8155-0 (pbk.)
— ISBN 978-1-4488-8161-1 (6-pack)
1. Popular music—Vocational guidance—Juvenile literature. I. Title.
ML3795.R418 2013
781.64023—dc23
                                   2012001529

Manufactured in the United States of America

CPSIA Compliance Information: Batch #B3S12WM: For Further Information contact Windmill Books, New York, New York at 1-866-478-0556

CONTENTS

TOO COOL FOR SCHOOL

Being a pop star is cool, right? What could be better than playing your favorite music as a job? If you can sing or play in a band, then you might dream of making it big.

⇨ American Idol winner Carrie Underwood sang at her local church as a child.

Is pop really for you?

Do you love music so much that you want to sing or play music all the time? If you want to be a pop star, you will have to practice every day. It's important to believe in yourself, too.

⇨ *Watching your favorite stars, such as will.i.am of the Black Eyed Peas, on TV can inspire you to aim for the top.*

CHOOSE YOUR ROLE

It's important to decide which role you want to take. Are you a singer or do you play an instrument? Do you want to be a solo star and sing on your own, or do you want to be in a band?

⬇ *Lady Gaga uses crazy costumes and wigs to help attract attention.*

IN THE SPOTLIGHT

Lady Gaga
Lady Gaga always wanted to be a pop star. She learned to play the piano when she was four years old. At 13 she wrote her first ballad (a song that tells a story).

Going solo

If you love singing and like to be the center of attention, you could be a solo act. Make sure you practice, it will be your voice that everyone hears!

⇧ *Join a band if you prefer being with other people to performing on your own.*

I'm in the band

If you want to play music, but don't want the spotlight on just you, try being in a band. You'll find friendship, lots of fun, and people to talk to about your music.

FIND YOUR STYLE

Some acts are "crossover acts." This means their music crosses over between styles, such as folk and **country**, and is liked by fans of both styles.

Talk about it

Lots of bands split up because the members of the band want to make different types of music. Talk to your band members about your favorite types of music. Try to agree on one of these styles:

- Pop
- Rock
- **Metal**
- **Rap**
- **Grunge**
- Dance
- Country

⇦ *You are more likely to be a pop star if you play the style of music you love best.*

Be yourself

Singing solo is harder than being in a band. You need to find a musical style of your own, instead of fitting in with a group. Learn what suits your voice. Can you sing a ballad or do high-energy dance tunes suit you better?

BE A STAR

Looking for ...
If you are looking for other members for your band, why not put an advertisement in your school magazine or on the bulletin board?

⬆ *All eyes will be on you if you're a solo star, so try to develop a strong image.*

SONGWRITING

Many of the artists who people respect the most don't just sing or play. They write their own songs, too.

Making a start

Some songwriters start by writing the words, or lyrics. They then add music. Your starting point might be a tune that you hum to yourself. Carry a notebook and pen so that you can write down any ideas or lyrics that you think of.

IN THE SPOTLIGHT

Singer-songwriters
Different styles of music have their own songwriting stars, from Beyoncé, Adele, and will.i.am to Taylor Swift. Look at their lyrics and listen to their music to learn how they put a good song together.

⬆ *Beyoncé is one of the most successful singer-songwriters in the world.*

What's in a song?

Popular songs are made up of different parts:

- **Chorus** (or refrain)
- **Bridge**
- **Key change**
- **Harmony**
- **Melody**
- **Rhythm**

Find out more about them on page 30.

⇨ *Taylor Swift was just 12 years old when she started writing her songs.*

SINGING STAR

From country stars to rock bands, all singers need to know how to sing so that they don't ruin their voice.

⬇ *If you want to be a rock singer, you'll need to take care of your voice.*

Stand up and sing! Standing in the correct position makes it easier for a singer to produce the right sounds. You should stand with your stomach in, chest out, shoulders back and down, chin up, feet slightly apart, and hands held loosely by your sides.

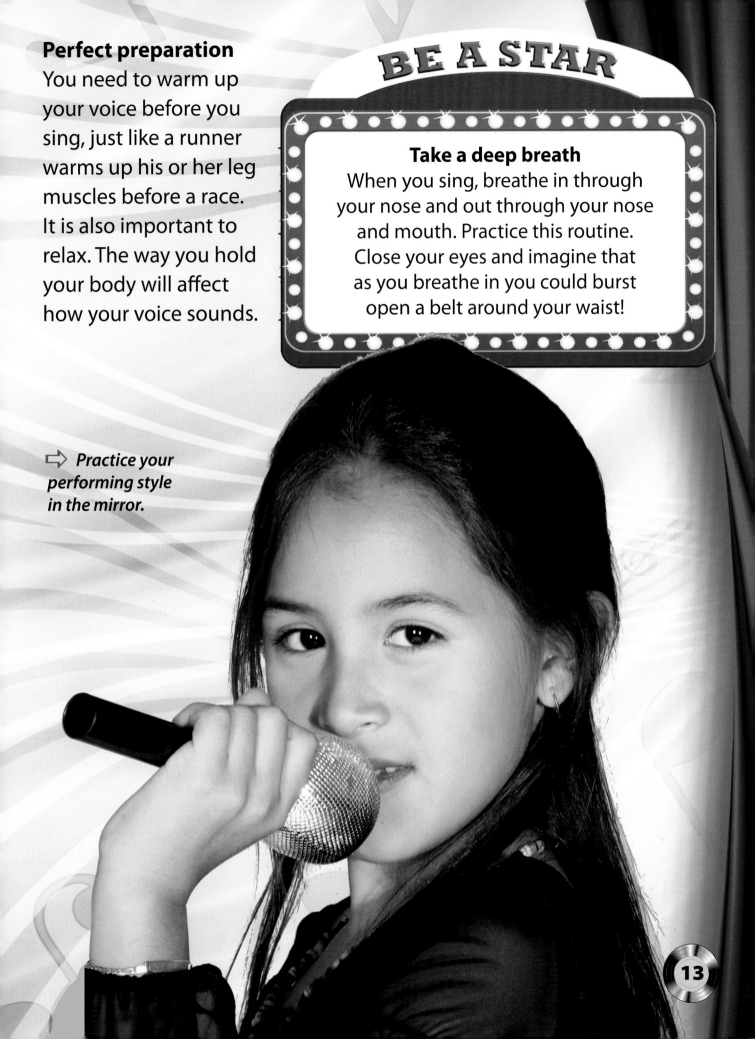

Perfect preparation

You need to warm up your voice before you sing, just like a runner warms up his or her leg muscles before a race. It is also important to relax. The way you hold your body will affect how your voice sounds.

BE A STAR

Take a deep breath
When you sing, breathe in through your nose and out through your nose and mouth. Practice this routine. Close your eyes and imagine that as you breathe in you could burst open a belt around your waist!

⇨ *Practice your performing style in the mirror.*

BUILD YOUR BAND

A band is often made up of a singer, a guitarist, a bassist (bass guitar player), and a drummer. Not all bands have these players, but building your band this way is a good way to start.

Finding each other

It's easy to form a band if you're from a musical family. This is how the Jonas Brothers and Kings of Leon got started. You may have friends who also want to be in a band. If you're struggling to find band members, ask friends and family. You'll be surprised how many people want to be in a band.

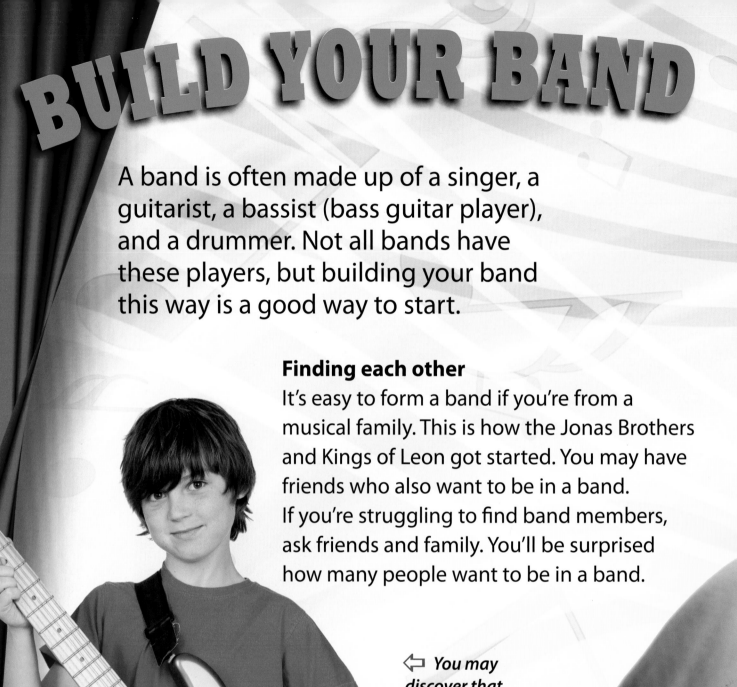

⇐ *You may discover that a friend loves playing guitar and wants to be in your band.*

IN THE SPOTLIGHT

No instruments needed!
You don't have to be able to play an instrument to be in a band. Groups such as the Pussycat Dolls sing and dance, but have no guitarist, drummer, or the other players usually found in a band.

⬇ *If you love playing piano, you could be the keyboard player in your band.*

PRACTICE, PRACTICE!

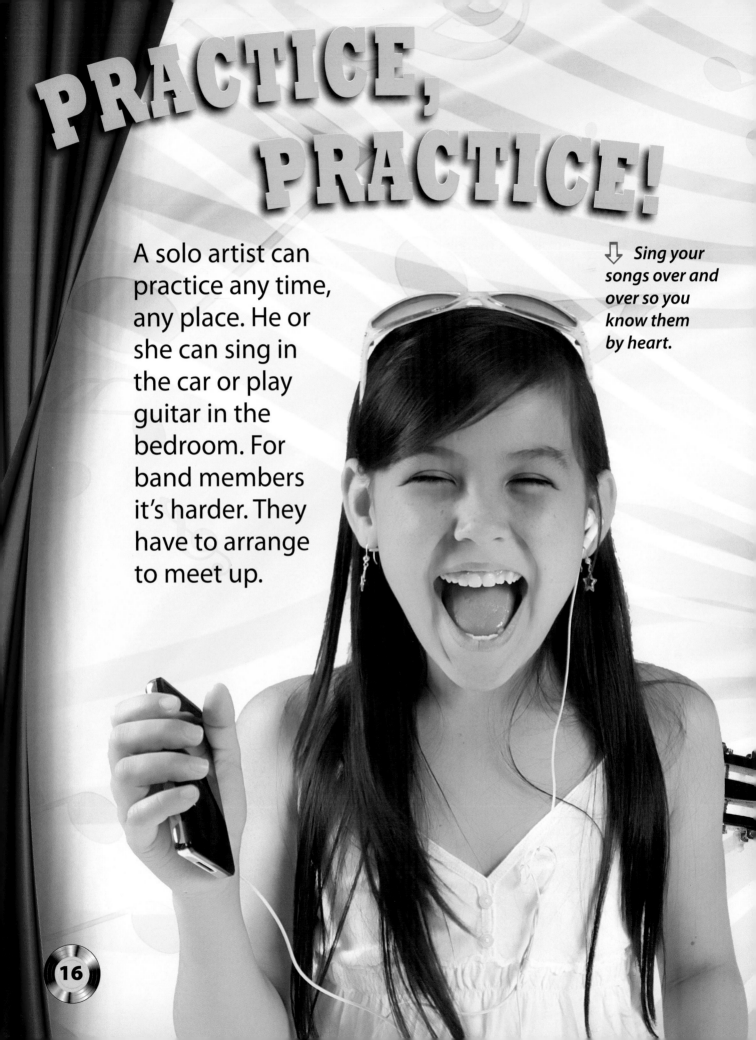

A solo artist can practice any time, any place. He or she can sing in the car or play guitar in the bedroom. For band members it's harder. They have to arrange to meet up.

⬇ *Sing your songs over and over so you know them by heart.*

⇩ Many bands have a guitarist who plays and also sings.

Borrow an instrument
Don't worry if you don't own an instrument. Lots of schools let kids borrow instruments to learn on. Your school may even have a space where you can rehearse.

Band practice
A band practice is called a rehearsal. One of the band members should arrange a time for the whole band to get together with their instruments and a list of what songs they are going to play.

Finding a space
Every band needs a rehearsal space. It should be large enough for all the band members and their instruments. It also needs to be somewhere where you won't disturb anyone else.

MOVE WITH THE MIC

Singing into a **microphone** makes your voice much louder. It comes naturally to some people, but others need to practice.

Hold on!

A microphone can be your best friend! If you feel scared in front of the crowd, you can always hold on tight to the mic. Do you dance and move around a lot as you sing? The mic stand is the point you always move back to, to take center stage.

⇨ *At first it might feel strange singing into a microphone, but you will soon get used to it.*

Hands free

If you do like to move and dance as you sing, you could wear a headset microphone. It clips into place over your head and stays in position no matter how many cool moves you make on stage!

Master the mic
Holding the mic 2 to 4 inches (5–10 cm) from your mouth gives the best results.

⬇ *Try to look at your audience when you sing, rather than at the microphone.*

ALL THE RIGHT MOVES

Some pop stars build their whole show around their voice and their songs. Many others add a "wow" factor with dance moves.

⇐ *You can show off some great moves during a guitar solo!*

Stealing the show

It's often the lead singer who grabs the attention because he or she can move freely while singing. It's harder to dance when you are playing the guitar, and just about impossible for a drummer, although it can be done! Check out Jimi Hendrix and AC/DC's Angus Young.

Dance routines

Even the best dancers arrange their dance moves before they hit the stage. If you are in a band, teach the same moves to all the singers, and even the guitarists, for a great display on stage.

IN THE SPOTLIGHT

Top performers
Watch a show by a top singer/dancer, such as Britney Spears, Lady Gaga, or Madonna. You'll be amazed by the number of costume changes, slick **backup dancers**, and high-energy routines.

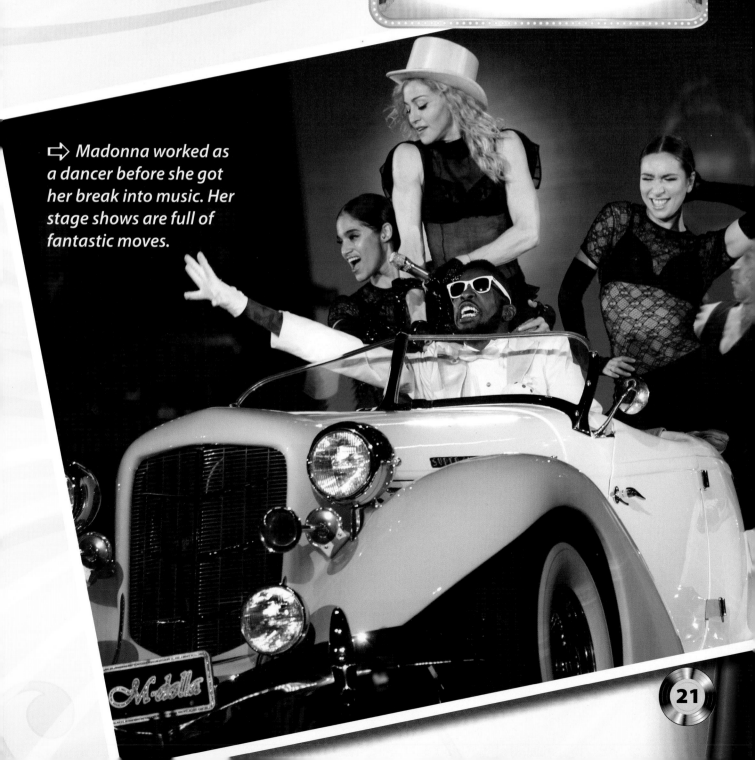

⇨ *Madonna worked as a dancer before she got her break into music. Her stage shows are full of fantastic moves.*

HIT THE STAGE!

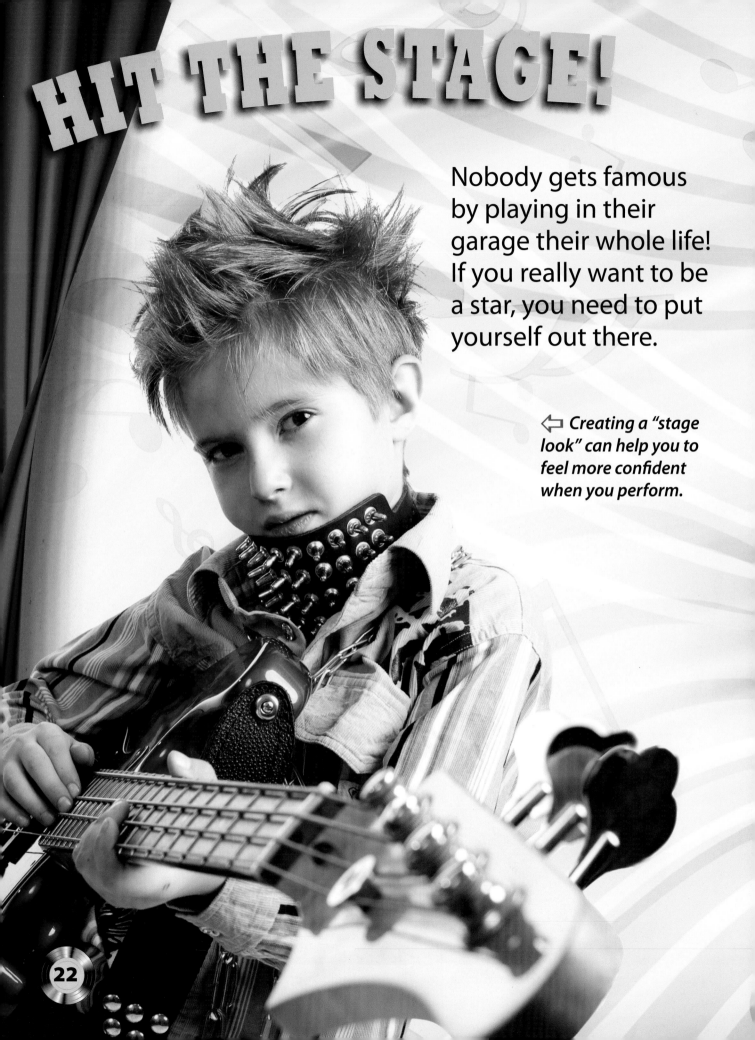

Nobody gets famous by playing in their garage their whole life! If you really want to be a star, you need to put yourself out there.

⇦ *Creating a "stage look" can help you to feel more confident when you perform.*

Playing for real

Take every chance you can to perform in public. Sing at school shows, talent contests, **karaoke** nights, or summer camp. Whether you're a rapper, a grunge guitarist, a country singer, or a punk act, you need to know what it's like to perform for a crowd.

Feeling nervous?

To get rid of nerves (feeling scared), close your eyes and breathe deeply. Imagine your breath is your favorite color. Think of that color coming in through your nose and going out through your mouth.

Stage fright

Most people feel scared before they walk out on stage in front of a crowd. The best way to get past this feeling is to just do it! Don't look at the whole crowd. Find a few faces at the front and take turns looking at each one.

⇐ *Britney Spears could sing confidently in front of an audience at the age of seven!*

23

FROM STUDIO TO GIG

If you have practiced until you're perfect, you may be ready to play in public (a gig) or record a song to give to other people. This type of recording is called a demo.

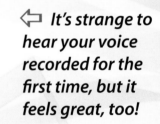

⇦ *It's strange to hear your voice recorded for the first time, but it feels great, too!*

Making a demo

You don't have to head for the recording studio to make a demo. Ask your music teacher or perhaps your parents or another family member to help. All you need is a little technical knowledge and some home equipment to record your music.

Getting a gig

Give your demo to people you know who might book you or your band. Make sure the CD has all your contact details on it. Include a short piece of writing about yourself or your band. If you can, include a photograph.

⇨ *Ke$ha spent her early years going to recording studios with her mom, who was a songwriter.*

SPREAD THE WORD

While you are trying to get a gig, or even a **recording contract**, spend time getting to know who your fans are and making more fans.

Internet-working

If your parents are happy with the idea, you could put yourself or your band on YouTube or another **social networking site**.

Tell everyone!

You could even make your own website. Tell all your friends to tell all their friends about your band. The more people you tell about your group, the more fans you are likely to have.

⇦ If you get to perform in public, ask all your friends to come and watch you play.

⇨ *The video for Justin Bieber's song "Baby" is the world's most viewed YouTube clip.*

Making contacts

Make friends with other musicians who might want to play with you. They may introduce you to people who have already booked them to play in public. You could stage a show with your friends' bands, and invite along anyone who might be able to help get you noticed.

IN THE SPOTLIGHT

YouTube talent

Justin Bieber was discovered when a talent manager saw his videos on YouTube.

HIT THE BIG TIME

If you are "spotted" by a record company or win a talent show, you'll still need to work very hard to stay at the top.

⬇ *Even when contestants have won American Idol, they have to work hard to keep their recording contracts.*

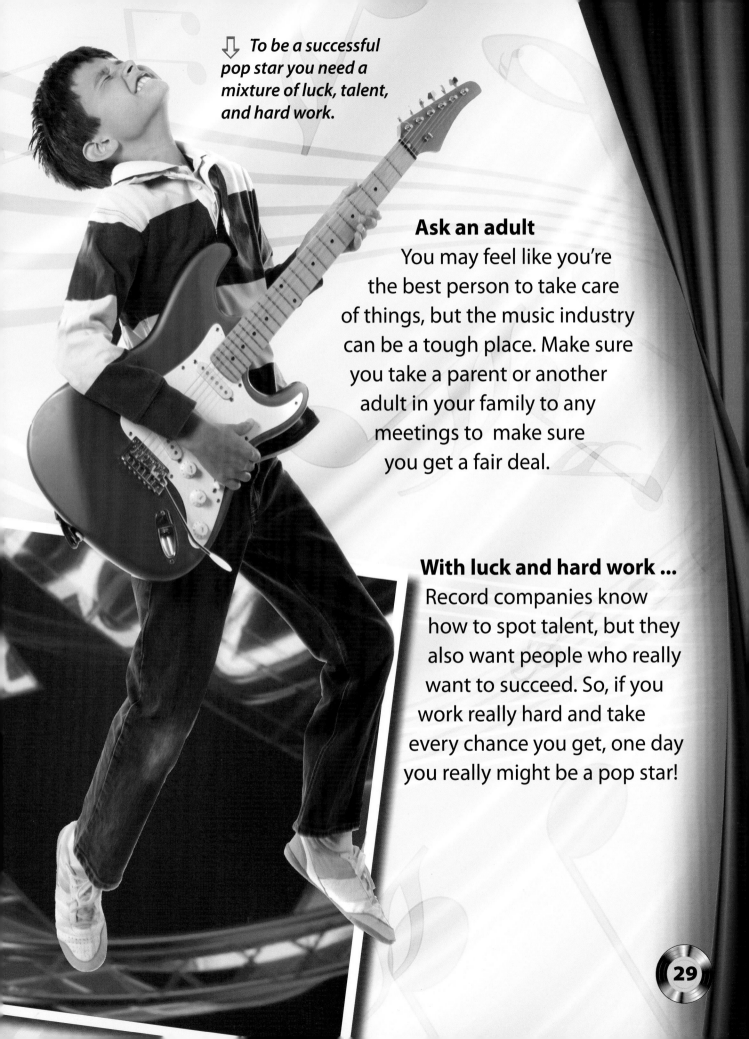

⬇ To be a successful pop star you need a mixture of luck, talent, and hard work.

Ask an adult

You may feel like you're the best person to take care of things, but the music industry can be a tough place. Make sure you take a parent or another adult in your family to any meetings to make sure you get a fair deal.

With luck and hard work ...

Record companies know how to spot talent, but they also want people who really want to succeed. So, if you work really hard and take every chance you get, one day you really might be a pop star!

GLOSSARY

backup dancers
(BAHK-up DANS-erz)
Dancer who dance with or
behind the lead artist.

bridge (BRIJ)
A part of a song, near the end,
that is different from the chorus
or the verses.

chorus (KAWR-us)
The lines of a song that are
repeated after each verse.
Also called a refrain.

country (KUN-tree)
A style of music that often includes
romantic or sad lyrics, and guitar,
banjo, or harmonica.

grunge (GRUNJ)
A style of music that combines rock
guitar with punk and metal.

harmony (HAR-muh-nee)
A note or notes played or sung
at the same time to make a
pleasing sound.

karaoke (kayr-ee-OH-kee)
Singing the lyrics of a song over the
song's background music.

key change (KEE CHAYNJ)
Moving from one musical key
to another.

melody (MEH-luh-dee)
A pattern of notes that make up
a tune.

metal (MEH-tul)
Short for heavy metal, it is a loud,
angry-sounding style of rock music.

microphone (MY-kruh-fohn)
An instrument used to record
sounds or to make sounds louder.

rap (RAP)
A style of music in which rhyming
words are spoken quickly over a
strong background beat.

recording contract
(rih-KAWR-ding KON-trakt) An
agreement between an artist and
a record company that the artist
will record a song and the record
company will sell it.

rhythm (RIH-thum)
A pattern of long and short
notes that is repeated during a
piece of music.

social networking site
(SOH-shul NET-wurk-ing SYT)
A website that people use to make
and keep in touch with friends.

FURTHER READING

Appice, Carmine. *Realistic Rock for Kids: Drum Beats Made Simple!*. Van Nuys, CA: Warner Brothers Publications/Alfred Music Publishing, 2002.

Cooke, C. W. *FAME: Pop Stars*. Vancouver, WA: Bluewater Comics, 2011.

Potts, Kimberly. *Kidz Bop: Be a Pop Star!: Start Your Own Band, Book Your Own Gigs, and Become a Rock and Roll Phenom!*. Avon, MA: Adams Media, 2011.

Schaefer, Adam R. *Forming a Band*. Rock Music Library. Mankato, MN: Capstone Press, 2004.

WEBSITES

For web resources related to the subject of this book, go to: www.windmillbooks.com/weblinks and select this book's title.

INDEX